rue Wilson Monday

Anselm Hollo

La Alameda Press :: Albuquerque

Some of these works have appeared in *Blue Book, Bombay Gin,*
Cybercorpse, First Intensity, Gare du Nord, Hanging Loose,
La Révolution Opossum (a.k.a. *Skanky Possum*), *murmur, Pharos,*
Prosodia, Samizdat, Sniper Logic, and *Sulfur.*

The author is grateful to the editors, publishers, printers,
and distributors of these publications.

Anselm Hollo and Jane Dalrymple-Hollo wish to acknowledge
the generosity of the Finnish Cultural Fund and the Grez-sur-Loing
Foundation of Gothenburg, Sweden, with the deepest gratitude:
"These organizations, and Mme Bernadette Plissart, the generous and
charming manager of the Hotel Chevillon in its present reincarnation,
made it possible for us to spend five serendipitous and productive
months in a version of Arcady. *rue Wilson Monday* is dedicated to
them, to our friends in France, and to the artists and poets of
France who have been a lifelong inspiration to both of us."

La Alameda Press
9636 Guadalupe Trail NW
Albuquerque, New Mexico 87114

6

Books by Anselm Hollo

POETRY
& It Is A Song
Faces & Forms
The Coherences
Haiku
Tumbleweed
Maya
Sensation 27
Some Worlds
Black Book
Notes & Paramecia
Lingering Tangos
Sojourner Microcosms
Heavy Jars
Lunch in Fur
With Ruth in Mind
Finite Continued
No Complaints
Pick Up the House
Outlying Districts
Space Baltic
Near Miss Haiku
Blue Ceiling
High Beam
West Is Left on the Map
Survival Dancing
Corvus
AHOE (And How on Earth)
AHOE 2 (Johnny Cash Writes
a Letter to Santa Claus)

ESSAYS
Caws & Causeries:
Around Poetry and Poets

SELECTED TRANSLATIONS
Poetry
Some Poems by Paul Klee
Red Cats
William Carlos Williams: Paterson
    (in German, with Josephine Clare)
Allen Ginsberg: Kaddisch und andere
    Gedichte (with J.C.)
Gregory Corso: Gasoline und andere
    Gedichte (with J.C.)
Paavo Haavikko: Selected Poems
Pentti Saarikoski: Selected Poems
The Poems of Hipponax
Pentti Saarikoski: Trilogy
Serious Poems: Kai Nieminen

Prose
Jean Genet: Querelle
Franz Innerhofer: Beautiful Days
Olof Lagercrantz: Strindberg
Peter Stephen Jungk: Werfel
Lennart Hagerfors: The Whales in
    Lake Tanganyika
Jaan Kross: The Czar's Madman
Rosa Liksom: One Night Stands
Lars Kleberg: Starfall: A Triptych

Plays & Screenplays
Bertolt Brecht: Jungle of Cities
Georg Büchner: Woyzeck
Francois Truffaut: Small Change
Louis Malle: Au revoir les enfants

To The School of Continuation

A Note

WHEN I WAS INVITED to spend five months in France, in an old hotel long frequented by artists and writers, I decided to write something that would NOT be your typical "sabbatical poem" — that familiar rumination, by the U.S. American academic (temporary) expatriate, "on" the Mona Lisa, Baudelaire's grave, or "how *different* all this is from back home in Missoula Montana!"

I believe that "rue Wilson Monday" turned out to be something possibly more interesting: A hybrid of day book, informal sonnet sequence (though more "simultaneist" than chronological), and extended, 'laminated' essay-poem. Works I found particularly inspiring in my endeavor were Ted Berrigan's *The Sonnets* and Edward Dorn's *Abhorrences* — books that will make me chuckle and weep to the end of my days.

The book received its title from French poet Guillaume Apollinaire's 1913 poem "Lundi rue Christine" (Monday rue Christine), a Cubist work composed almost entirely out of verbatim speech from various conversations in a cafe.

In "rue Wilson Monday," similar conversations take place in and around my head during that stay (August 1998 / January 1999) at the Hotel Chevillon, an artists' and writers' retreat in the small town of Grez-sur-Loing. Back in 1876, Robert Louis Stevenson came to visit his cousin Robert at this hotel, whose present street address is 114 rue Wilson, "La Rue Grande" (Main Street) back then. There he met Fanny Osbourne, the woman he was to pursue across the Atlantic and the North American continent and eventually marry.

Thus, "Cousin Bob" and "Cousin Louis" put in appearances in this book, as do Charlie Chaplin, Heraclitus, Utah Phillips, Beatrice Portinari, William Holden, Ted Berrigan, Guido Cavalcanti, John Lennon, Bill Clinton, Robert Bly, William Burroughs, Petrarch's Laura, Stéphane Mallarmé, Ben Jonson, Tom Raworth, Aleksandr Herzen, Gertrude Stein, Archy the Vers Libre Cockroach, Oscar Wilde, Damien Hirst, The White Goose of Grez, and a whole bunch of others you may or may not have heard of.

To invite the reader to participate in my often elliptical conversations with these folks, I have provided footnotes, and these too are an integral part of the poem and the conversation.

Boulder, Colorado
3 January 2000 C.E.

Those crepes were great
The tap is running

GUILLAUME APOLLINAIRE

"Monday rue Christine"

1

carriage purrs man whistles pounds post
in distant rocky dark
reason, weaving, brabbles
cognition digs tunnel through Charlot's suitcase
zoom cog motion   seagull cry
arms around everything
parallel out of someone
else's heaven tunnels
behind doors past
lit-up, frontal, still convinced
climb reviewed
now cautious move to igloo syntax
doodle on   smoke
watch reflections flounce

Charlot: French nickname for Charlie Chaplin in early silent movies.

2

beautiful thoughts
beware of those who write to write beautiful thoughts
upper limit: poet as brain in jar
lower limit: poet as hectoring moralistic asshole
prefer the difficile   the delicately unstable
sealed & farouche   or gamesome pasquinade
but faced with such stirring
Mister Intellectual Rigor marches back in
a staunchly secular sort of guy
deep bits of sky begin to beat
wave summons to water
bird is also just bird said dragonfly
but now there's a kind of drone   card in wrong slot
bits of rough bark fall off trunk

difficile: "hard to deal with, stubborn, unreasonable" (English);
"difficult" (French). farouche: "marked by shyness and a lack
of social graces" (English); "wild, fierce, shy" (French).
pasquinade: publicly posted lampoon, satire — from "Pasquino,"
remains of ancient statue excavated in Rome in 1501, on which
people posted satirical compositions in bad Latin.

3

that thar wind is
really movin'
them thar clouds along
what crowing eccentricity made me write that
well now how about the past
past tense of climb   i.e. "clomb"?
CLOMB (an insert):
clomb to the cave
where midget brigands
used to stash
their big false mustachios
wrote this with my French "Red Arrow" pen
& the geese they's a-honkin' down by the river Loing
sounding like Kirby Malone   pronouncing "bain"

"crowing eccentricity": not a typo. Kirby Malone: noted
Baltimore poet/performance artist.

4

the stuff of the psyche is a smoke-like substance
says Heraclitus   it is constantly in motion
only movement can know movement ah
this be head-sensitive material
forever in deep shade
we get together to make noises at each other
when we're not there we miss those noises
but hey boss isn't it time to lighten up says archy
you old opsimath you what's that it's one who learns
things late in life & when has it not been
'late in life,' si vales bene est ego valeo
beloved beasts open to so many
'interpretations' we or awe, as in aw shucks
if you are well that is good I am well too

Heraclitus quotes, here as elsewhere, from Guy Davenport's
translation. archy: Don Marquis' vers-libertarian cockroach.

5

once again butterfly pulse entire percept
fictional jolt of eye: arms, yarns
hit me adventure come kiss me sadness
as if me had me still
in this ocean of "socio-political & aesthetic"
idiot electric catacomb gibberish
tumbling billows of stuff
something there is in man
wants to be top big banana baboon
but I am not Robert Frost I am a baboon
mad about the planet   even this week
in the America that was   it had that phrasing
ecstatic articulate and beaucoup
beaucoup conscious disquiet

6

now does the blissful somnambule recluster
a dream a flesh-colored dream? say what?
how to identify the ones who tend to war
& what to do about them   discuss
on different color paper free up text
from fuzzy spaces inside head. hey,
are these walls "of" someplace? he stood
a veteran user of mind's ear
for tales of The Device
mortals love noise hurled into gaping flesh
well maybe yes. roll eyes round écriture
distortion makes you enemies
so either "say" things or it's endless postpreface
the elsewhere gunfire problem whose is it

écriture: writing (Fr.).

7

"the ideal story is that of two people
who go into love   step for step
with a fluttered consciousness
like a pair of children venturing together
into a dark room" yeah right but then
then it's LIGHTS! CAMERA! ACTION!
& the relentless Surroundarama
Split-Screen Spectacle of
Everyday Life   & Things to Do
but it's still a terrific idea
since being what or who is also just with
in days & nights of beaucoup conscious disquiet
though sometimes it's not so easy
to reinsert oneself   into the mortal coil

"the ideal story . . .": Robert Louis Stevenson.

8

the general infantilization
that became a groundswell of our century (said Eva)
not that we weren't part of it
when we were young & cruel
"deny yourself nothing"   well that's one theory
only the creature knows its awful secret joys
and the mobile digressive figments collide (said Ann)
and people don't read
poetry because uncertainty
is associated with punishment (said Mark)
is stupid attention better than no attention
what about hissing a poem   instead of the usual
soulful quaver or well-rehearsed scream
when your memory goes forget it (said Utah)

"Eva" — Eva Hesse, Pound's German translator, essayist.
"Ann" — Ann Lauterbach. "Mark" — Mark Wallace.
"Utah" — Utah Phillips. Great singers all.

9

yes tribe so richly rhymes with diatribe
but voice in you is home, please give us brains!
Mr. Meter, meet Mr. Foot
the voice in you is home
"thou art too elliptical"
but what's not foible anymore?
farewell Bay Area it's been unreal
now text participants will perform
a simultaneous vote of thanks
so get thee to the poem office
before time goes antique
on seascape's rainy nakedness
(spoken in cóntent absolutely)
how sings her my head such uncanny apples

10

most beautiful order of the world
still just a random gathering of things
insignificant in themselves
says Heraclitus
but man's bootstraps, his imagination
is quite a part of reality
says Larry Eigner   and history
will be revisionist   ALL history
WILL be revisionist   all power temporal
power exists in TIME
"your time is up, Mr. Power"
and there he goes
with all his little
longings & belongings   there he goes

11

gates waterfalls shifting horizons
plastic halberds gentle fugitives
una Beatrice on the ramparts of Carcassonne
in black miniskirt more like Juliette Greco
is she thinking of "Raymond the Cathar Count of Toulouse"
fat chance she's gazing at sudden
flock of paragliders in the sky
while the guide drones on & I think of
"fictitious employment by no means uncommon in France"
he means government employment
fictitious government employment
but then government is fictitious too
as are the governed much of the time
look for yourself in this pebble or pencil

12

the only good knee   is a live knee
(how incontestably true)
& we do be fond of these limbs that take us
across lands old & new & enormous waters
(which at times make one feel a bit like a vole
facing infinity)   & return us to calmer things
"oriented" "at home" simply just where it is
(draped over her shoulder   green eyes confident:
"we are going to the studio!")
or "the study of gratifying discourse"
(inscription on Chinese scholar's cottage
two hundred years ago)
the way the waters' voices speak
slow erudite surprises   yarns in your arms

"draped over her shoulder" — Zophiel the Cat, who stayed
in Boulder, Colorado and was much missed at rue Wilson.

13

just where it is is with you
whom I found fifteen years ago
empty & sad I was   as one of Simenon's tales
pretty much heading across the river & into the trees
(my particular brand of sentimentality)
a wanderer twixt the two worlds
of Bar Trance & Brain Tundra   reluctant to dance
not even in the manner of William Holden in Picnic
but who can tell the story of true astonishment
not even Guido who did try   but with him I say
that I saw in my lady's eyes a light
that brought a new spirit into my heart
"awakening there a cheerful life"
— so, Happy Birthday, Janey! signed: Yours, Biped Al.

"not even in the manner of William Holden in Picnic": how
Ted Berrigan once described his dancing style. Guido:
Cavalcanti. "awakening there a cheerful life": "sì che vi
desta d'allegrezza vita" (Mark Cirigliano's translation).
"Biped Al": a "spell-check" donnée (fortuitous present).

14

now does he know how to beam? contented?
grow fuzzy? nothing wrong with fuzzy
blissful? feel some place
keep stupid demons at bay
let them go or go on
hammering nothing in Nothing Land —
this be quite different
from crazy hot soul of sudden beginnings
cluttered & ever 'novel' inside
yes that did make for impetuous bellows
violent staggerings   irritating ruins
before it all settled into rose debris;
so locate old hotel before books close
on trundling troubadours. semicolon

15

give up your ampersands & lowercase 'i's
they still won't like you
the bosses of official verse culture
(U.S. branch)   but kidding aside
I motored off that map a long time ago
yet have old friends
still happily romping in the English lyric
and Reverdy! dear Reverdy! so much of him rhymes
it must be   poésie   ma chérie ...
looks at the stacks of books on the floor
gods help us, dear poets
pass the salt pass the mustard
hike the present
or the hypothetically honest horse-drawn past

16

bygone masks of the night: dream, sentence, voices, air
undulating desire   but then what was there for lunch
"MOOTHWATERING HAMBURGUERS"?
do we take it the basic unit of "the new poem"
is the menu? OK I'll take it
one flight down with a daffodilly
for my love
& if that's too silly
I'll hit myself over the head with my billy
club   o let the chemicals bubble
when this you see you see a PANEL
of edited accidents   "cumshaw"   cumshaw?
"small gift offered in thanks or as inducement, gratuity"
now isn't all this just too atrocious

"MOOTHWATERING HAMBURGUERS" — sign outside fast-food
restaurant in Palma de Mallorca. "cumshaw" — kam sia:
Xiamen dialect, port in SE China: "grateful thanks."
Entered English in early 1800's.

17

draped in defiance & bewildered hair
not up to the waves of the task
ready for the big mallet   yet still chanting
"what vast sky wagons? what balloon yard?
what order to this?"
praying for door back to scale
begin the beguine may body begin
to turn the big barrel climb mountain
regain some sense of basic human
ever esurient for flash of meaning
our minds too orderly
in ways too predictable
so fill in the blank
between fedora and wingtip shoes

esurient — exhibiting hunger or greediness (Latin *esurire*
= to be hungry).

18

as we glance out from our machine
time leaps ahead, slips away
into clumsy but sensitive entity's
invisible notebooks   but imagination
consists of desire   "professional desire —
it lit me, by god   from heavy top to toe"
who was that now was it my dear
irrational suspect, Perennially Dangerous
Adolescent? maybe however some'a dese young'uns
a bit too 'techno' for jaded old taste
(rolls back down, perplexed
by field of too much stuff)
ah short meander best meander
verbarium empty, once again

19

certainly privileged to have an
interior existence one likes
well . . . doesn't mind? sometimes even enjoys?
hard not to be bored by oneself
just another incoherent refugee
once radical high and true   oh long ago
in pow! pow! converse
been there   what's the rush   wipe the screen
sway deep shade, opaque   bleak lacunae for sure
wrinkly, repeatable   thought to rip up
the book of small odes but was again charmed
by its miniature world so couldn't do it no
couldn't do it   now back to think on
idealized historical conduct vs. tendresse

tendresse: tenderness (Fr.)

20

came down the old oaken stairs he must also have trod
who wrote "old and young, we are all on our last cruise"
and "to know what you like is the beginning of wisdom
and of old age" or up those stairs again, to read: "the old
appear in conversation in two characters:
the critically silent
and the garrulous anecdotic"   Cousin Louis
who first met his Fanny here   thanks to Cousin Bob
who was the more dashing   the model for Alan Breck
and perhaps the dark Master of Ballantrae
when first we came here in August the pigeons next door
said coo-COO coo-coo   coo-COO coo-coo
but now in November it's only coo-coo-COO
coo-coo-COO   so, time to go, soon

21

oft turning others' leaves
calm is the sea; the waves work less and less
oh that my heart could hit upon a strain
would strike the music of my soul's desire
what joy seems half so rich from rapture won
as the loud laugh of maidens in the sun
when selfish greed becomes a social sin
the world's regeneration may begin
now slides the silent meteor on
shake hands forever my silly ghost
desire! desire, I have too dearly bought
with price of mangled mind thy worthless ware
an endless wind doth tear the sail apace
it is some picture on the margin wrought

Composed out of lines by Philip Sidney, Henry Howard,
Nicholas Breton, John Clare, Ada Cambridge, Alfred Tennyson,
Michael Drayton, Thomas More, William Drummond,
and Thomas Wyatt.

22

"that the ants seem to wobble
as the morning sun catches their shadows"
not with us "too much" at all
not with us very long at all   the sun the ants
the wobbling shadows   all too hung up we be
on a civilization devoted to the speechless stare
punctuated by mindless speech
(& WHO is likely to read
these headthrob grumblespeak lyrics?)
"because they do not understand that cacophony
is at least as intricate an art   as harmony"
& she cries out in her dream "where are you going?"
infinitesimal moods for milliseconds
kindly provide a theme for   these variations

"that the ants seem to wobble / as the morning sun catches their shadows"
— EP, Canto LXXX, p. 105 in *The Pisan Cantos* (London: Faber & Faber,
1949). "because they do not understand that cacophony is at least as intricate
an art as harmony" — Basil Bunting, "The Lion and the Lizard," p. 30 in
Three Essays (Durham: Basil Bunting Poetry Centre, 1994).

23

"I wish that life were an opera
I should like to live in one"
said Stevenson, Robert Louis
& les Surréalistes du Mid-Ouest
showed up at a reading
by the Reverend Robt. Bly   in Chicago
to (at least momentarily) estop
his woodnotes wild
with a large, vigorously &
accurately propelled
cream pie
"beauty will be convulsive" et cetera yes chérie
we must needs beg to differ with rare Ben
& let the Lybian lion hunt them butterflies

"les Surréalistes du Mid-Ouest" — "the Surrealists of the Midwest."
They know who they are. Last two lines refer to Ben Jonson's
"the Libyan lion hunts no butterflies" (To a Friend, an Epigram of Him).

24

only & always as old as who I'm talking to, no, with
then, how old am I when talking myself? to? with?
pondering practical martial origins of various ferocities
of man way past brain   that dark reviewed
tunnel doodles out of cognition igloo
thus head learns fictions
material life & arms o.k. but am I a dream
hurled & become a figment in groundswell
a noise of things settling on shelves
prattling selves   quavered elliptics
history shifting, sudden, us too
"surf's up, mister!"   o.k. I kill trees
it's barrel time, dear   time to watch
poppy fields billow in staunch wind

25

faintly flapping horizon of Symbolist project
fused in cosmic azure (French pronunciation)
brief clouds merge and pass
away away   into other vapors
"Hyperbole! from my mémoire
Triumphantly you rise today, grimoire"
ah, Stéphane Mallarmé
after a lifetime in classroom hell
translated Poe, but his students
never learned any English
neither did two of mine who attempted
yet another translation of the dice-toss
enshrined now   in exalted lacquer box
we have to think French to read him

"grimoire" — "a) piece of mumbo jumbo; illegible scrawl; unreadable
scribble; b) magician's book of spells" (Collins-Robert French/English
Dictionary). "in exalted lacquer box" — Mallarmé shared Whistler's and
Manet's love of Japanese art and artifacts.

26

crackle crackle "good" "history"?
verify tales of each ego?
crackle crackle cerebral twitch
who slipped on the caviar?
who broke the hammer clavier?
& that was by Stupid Staggering Desirée
(Jean Baudrillard's favorite group) (who he?)
(I think he invented The Meter)
(well take him back to the meter office)
& that is so bad it's really kinda great
crackle crackle screeches whistles & ululations
(you say communists, bro? those really happen?)
hand me the righteous indignation   but first
let me negotiate this corniche

corniche — road built along cliff-lined coast.

27

walls dwellings built, streets paved
with stones from old ruined fortress
rue Wilson was the Grande Rue
first came modernism of subject matter
then came modernism of form(s)
followed by wiseass postmodernism
present company not excluded
those crepes were great
the tap is running
the lights just went out where are the candles
did we take some candles on board Mr Bosun
aye aye Captain Dustball
but no land in sight it's a long haul
to daffodil land and galactopoiesis

"those crepes were great / the tap is running" — translation of this
book's epigraph. "galactopoiesis" — pertaining to
the secretion of milk; but perhaps, and why not, to a "galactic poetics"?

28

lover walks out on friend   what a mosquito!
other friend almost dies in fire
"the phone was busy   so I was sure he was there"
firemen would not believe it at first
she insisted   he was brought out
greeted her with big smile a week later
totally wired hooked up still unable to speak
surrounded by terror we are yes indeedy
days of rocket up then straight down
when the good times don't roll no mo'
or they don't roll the way they used to
"Fings Ain't Wot They Used to Be"
sunny afternoon, London: Mr. Norman & Mr. Corso
imbibing Scotch in my study   Big Bad Boys Together

"Mr. Norman & Mr. Corso": the late Frank Norman, ex-convict,
author of "Fings Ain't Wot" etc., successful East End musical directed
by Joan Littlewood in the late Sixties; and Gregory the Herald.

29

in fragile days on frightful parapet
space sustains quest! eat art, Stéphane!
inside a stagecoach don your cuirass
sink into head's reanimated folds
torsos anthologized by gaze in days
of . . . thin black wind streaks into machine:
"space light on pocket students . . . dig
joker dolly idol dirge censor . . . moose dada
maw finery nada soggy moan . . .
a-and as for my favorite christians
they're Fletcher Christian
Linda Christian   and The Magic Christian"
thanks Bill   now inscribed in grimoire
not easily deciphered by Proud to Be Dumb & Brawny School

"eat art, Stéphane" — Mallarmé, of course, who not only ate and drank
it but was art. "thanks, Bill" — William S. Burroughs. Quite a treat,
to have both these guys on the same page.

30

stalking the elusive ego? a bit like gravity
no one's ever seen one
nor do we really know how it works
"Vous etes Américain?" "Oui —
de l'Amérique de John Lennon"
geese honk on river, moped kids roar by
people are fond of the world's smallest dogs
a low-slung wire-haired bottlebrush kind
that likes to wear its eyes completely covered
since it can't really see anything anyway
& we've been here for years
wow, or "pouf!," as they say here
years like they used to make
not present souped-up blur-speed corporate model

"Vous êtes Américain?" "Oui — de l'Amérique de John Lennon."
— "You're American?" "Yes — from John Lennon's America."
"& we've been here for years" — de facto, five months.

31

steer resolutely into the Dada channel
but hoist old pre-Raph flag now & again
as in "those lovely days of youth
when so often we thought
we'd die from laughing together"
wrote Madame Sévigné   those days are here and now
more than ever they were in my belle jeunesse
swans either dignified or hilarious
when upside down looking for alimentation
blue heron swoops overhead   blessings so many
ways beyond 'counting'   long had we sought
for nutts amid the shade   & though we're all busy
in this world building towers of Babel said Cousin Louis
life is a permanent possibility of sensation

"pre-Raph" — pre-Raphaelite. "belle jeunesse" — literally
"beautiful youth": the original quote in French is "Cette
belle jeunesse où nous avons souvent pensé crever de rire
ensemble." "long had we sought for nutts amid the shade"
— John Clare, *Nutting*. "Cousin Louis"— R.L. Stevenson.

32

now for some questions about As I Was Saying:
was As I Was Saying a pseudonym for Major Dustball?
or was he a member of the Cacademy of Amurkan Poets?
was As I Was Saying known? known to whom? known in France?
was As I Was Saying a positive profane development
(like "pie-ganism" in the UK)?
or was he just a fake jesus on horseback in buckskins
(like Buffalo Bill)?
was As I Was Saying a diffident dissident? a syllabubus?
a synopopsis? a fraggyloductus?
was As I Was Saying pumped full of vitamins,
ready to roll on the Eurostar?
where did he come from, this As I Was Saying?
where did he go?

"a fraggyloductus" — dream language; semantic signfication unknown.

33

waiting   waiting for a loved one to return
waiting for air raid sirens
waiting as in the old French popular song
"J'attendrai"   waiting   repeating the word
boring as waiting can be   "Bored Again"
nice anti-fundamentalist bumper sticker
and so time curls slowly around
yet another bad anecdote   blue hour
a look both frightened and brave yes
we can make things fall from the sky
post-USA poets will ponder our programming
& its consequences in the third millennium
"remote ends are a dream" said Alex
the one with heart in his name

"said Alex" — Aleksandr Herzen: 1812-70, Russian revolutionary
leader and writer. "Herz": German for "heart".

34

be serious yes
can you / can't you be serious
yes and no
"the only important thing is to be
somebody's favorite composer"
come on somebody let me give you a hug
then let's sneak away
from old fill-in-the-blank school rhythms
on a ship in a storm
you're not going to wait for the verb
& when they asked the member of the English department
if there were any poets in the department:
"They don't have elephants
in the zoology department, do they?"

"the only important thing . . . ": "I remember what [John] Cage once
said to me when I was a very young man and looked him up for
tutoring and advice. He asked me what I wanted with my music,
and when I did not know what to answer, he asked me if I wanted to
be a respected composer. Somewhat confused I answered, yes,
I suppose so. Then he said, don't try that, the world is full of respected
composers that nobody cares about. The only important thing is to be
somebody's favorite composer." — Sten Hanson, Swedish poet &
composer (member of Fylkingen group), in "Word Score Utterance
Choreography," eds. Bob Cobbing & Lawrence Upton, London: Writers
Forum, 1998. "on a ship in a storm" — my father, J.A. Hollo, on the
comparative merits of English vs. German. "& when they asked"
— thanks to Don Byrd for the anecdote.

35

scurry down bleak corridors in Gare du Cauchemar
conflicting arrows point to a spot in the floor
this is the way to your train, left, no, right
straight down, no, straight up
so, my dear, you'll just have to ROCKET out of here
as will the entire species in three hundred years
has someone said this before you? not to worry,
they'll do so again and there's no reason whatever
for this to be fourteen lines
or lines at all, come to think of it
right now I just want to get home to my desk
to translate another play of drab awfulness
which on the evidence of a show of "new art" we just saw
is the esthetic of these pretentious boonies

"Gare de Cauchemar" — "Nightmare Station," more specifically,
the Gare de Lyon in Paris. "show of 'new art'" — piles of rugs roped
together; overblown photographs of nothing much; the umpteenth
thousandth 'minimalist' surface . . .

36

and there was the 'art opening' in Moret
old gutted church floored with gravel
we were taken on a tour of the two young women's works
everyone stopping to listen to detailed explications
(French pronunciation) with copious quotes and references
to the works of French thinkers
spoken at levels of animation and velocity quite beyond
our capacity to follow
assembled Moretians classically polite & attentive
that was a year ago   we twinkled at each other   still do
though there have been times not so twinkly this year
once again season turns leaves tumble off trees
once again happy birthday dear favorite painter
whose work speaks for itself!   and sings, and dances, too

37

consider "considerate"
best not to consider it too much
what was I after? the Colossus of Rhodes?
always adored   the mouse that roared
in zee canyons of Nueva York
gosh yes as the man said writing
allows you to weep and laugh all by yourself
& yes why not "chart the power codes" too
don't you wish you knew who I'm talking to
or that I did or they did
oh she was just a little colossus
moaning in the dark   "it was so dark
in Sarvan Vistay"   but sky over Baghdad
's now lit up again by expensive explosives

"writing allows you to" — Ramón Gomez de la Serna, "Greguerías".
"it was so dark" — line from a Swedish poet his co-translator Gunnar
Harding and I used to giggle about back in the seventies.

38

returns, twilight-summoned, the master of dolorous speak
now click here for dazzling version of nothing
but hearts moated by joyful pessimism
sing with watery creatures, sleep in leaky boats
curtains on eyelids, dark laughter heard falling
out over ivy, with music, cut to tracer bullets
earth trembles under mysterious house on Closed Eyes Road
closed form is coffin, Pentagon is closed form
expensive explosives engulfed by fracturing stone
punctuate swarm of questions, "it's all opaque"
watch the cerebral thermometer disintegrate
globules of mercury, angle of hand on keyboard
sparks of silence & nonsense fly up the chimney
longing: a kind of loitering, with no intent

"it's all opaque" — Basil Bunting, in print and conversation.
"longing: a kind of loitering" — response to Thomas A. Clark's
"longing is a kind of lingering."

39

no "word count" in poetry
there used to be a "line count"
but nowadays even that
's become a little dubious   what's a "line"?
is it just pieces?
yes it's just bits and pieces
did G.A. Custer's ghost
flit through their conversation
(Fanny and Louis at Grez)?
but even so   a change
from the world as murder & alimentation
cats eat birds birds eat worms worms eat us
between words   silence
in the silence   a face

This poem consists of seventy-five words, arranged on
fourteen lines. "did G.A. Custer's ghost": Robert Louis
Stevenson met his wife-to-be Fanny Osbourne in the village
of Grez-sur-Loing in July 1876, not long after Custer met
La Muerte at the Greasy Grass on June 25. So, the answer
is, presumably, yes.

40

how about just a few words
decoratively arranged on the page
with plenty of espace
between them around them
above and below, in good old
Mallarméan flotation mode?
lids on houses   mist over arches
of invisible speech to cast more light
"keylight?" on human window
thread of night   flash of jasmin
chickadee in the rain
away from guard rail identity
and all those bloody nations
in their implacable hats

"espace" — space (Fr.).

41

rare bright sunny December day in the Isle of France
WHY do I sit here & worry about a dead friend's book
due out 2 months ago? and WHO
are these hulks at cave mouth
waiting for brains to catch up with their stomachs? *)
flashed on a screen of ciel as bleu as my laptop's
"your query was all noise words, or blank
please make sure that at least one word
in your query is not a noise word"
but that was how we first summoned
faint image of life from dour spark
'noise words' relate things to one another
"because before between but" yes! BUT! & yes, BECAUSE!
*) probably right-wing members of United States Congress

"Isle of France" — Île de France, the administrative department
surrounding Paris. "ciel" — sky, "bleu" — blue (Fr.).

42

streets of water sadness, self's knotty beast
and its unreadable mysteries
wrapped in above head, pilgrim of empty air
on days of pale silhouettes grappling through past
certain wor(l)ds have elusive time
it is what gets gazed upon
against the sky
but now move in on the question
beyond pages squandered
on long gone mirrors, memory coins
treacherous operettas
now say hand, street, soul
say friendly vegetable, profile of cat
summer tobacco, circling birds

43

In the jingle-jangle mornings I went following you
& you & you & you   (a love letter to the word "and")
"You see here before you," Guillaume said, "me"
Laments, Consolations   And what is not a quotation?
"Words, m'dear, words, not pretty pictures"
The leaves are detaching themselves
Letting gravity do its job
Go ahead, read Mr. Rumi, read Mr. Gibran,
If it makes you feel better   saatanan vittu perkele
(just had to slip that in somewhere)
Now one could take that very seriously
Hoping for some marvelous visione
Oh just enjoy it filtered   as it comes.
"Best oatmeal," said Harry Smith, "I ever had!"

"saatanan vittu perkele" — roughly, Finnish equivalent of
"sh*t p*ss f*ck hell." visione: vision (It.) Harry Smith —
the filmmaker, musicologist, magus, collector of cat's cradles
and many other things. "Best oatmeal" — at Marie's on
North Broadway, Boulder, Colorado. With Allen Ginsberg,
another dear ghost.

44

time and desire their offspring devour
in heaven's forgetful snooze
that's from The Paleface Love Call Waltz
excuse me but which English are we now speaking
there's a poet writes these little machines
I must admit I quite like them
partly because I remember his smile
it is a nice smile   a famous smile
but right now I'm reading a French book of poems
in which the only proper noun is Raworth
"la lune noire de Raworth est rectangulaire"
so Tom has a dark moon? and it's rectangular?
hmm   specific weights of words different
in French poetic lexical table of elements

"la lune noire de . . . " — from Claude Royet-Journoud,
Les natures indivisibles (Paris, Gallimard 1997). Claude
is not the poet referred to in the preceding lines, although
he, too, has a very nice smile.

45

some of the French no longer writing poems like that
celebrate the new year by trying to kill some birds
then silence swells   the product picks someone
democracy sinks   are we legends of grace?
who wanted to know that, what did you order,
who purchased these herbs   whom have the fires eaten?
the director turns   "I must rule someone"
his umbrella a rose
the bank of his thought so unique a barrel
under a desk in the desert
between the jungle and the head
between this need and some other
falls the pleasure operator's
whisper: a valve of wonder

46

and these may well be
"snippets of impossible interiority"
"and that certain images be formed in the mind
                              to remain there"
"or the bugs in Mrs. Jevons' hotel"
or coots, "foulques," small black diver birds
that rocket up   then straight down
on the pond near Grez
                    whence came the town's building stones
yes time is a voice goes a-roaming
on those soirées that leave small holograms
in the old brain cellos
(and no, that is not a typo,
even though first thought was cells)

"snippets of . . .": from a review of another poet's book by
Steve Evans. "and that certain images . . .": Ezra Pound,
Pisan Cantos, p. 30. "or the bugs . . .": ibid., p. 32.

47

and where is FORTUNE DUBOISGOBEY
woke up this morning to his echoing name
"author of sensational novels
with titles like 'The Severed Hand'
whose works occupy many columns
of the British Library catalogue"
the dusty rat barrel Paradiso of books
that were meant to be read fast
they were written fast   & they were gone real fast
EMILE GABORIAU! XAVIER DE MONTEPIN!
"in moments of effort one learns to do
the easy things people like"
said Cousin Louis who was a fan of those guys
they worked so hard   and so fast

Information on 19th century French pop authors from Louis
Stott's "Robert Louis Stevenson & France" (Milton of
Aberfoyle, Creag Darach Publications, 1994).

48

now back to States whose President
is bullied by the viciously lame
  — cultural demons, embodied in ignorant power heads
                    (sadly, including his own) —
into facing sex mores Inquisition
unable to tell them "That, you sanctimonious slugs,
is none of your business!"
as the Scot poet psychologist who died playing tennis
once told innocent questioner plagued by internal rakshasas:
"Just tell them to FOCK OFF!"
watch out in the lands of fanatical hypocrites
smiling, unsmiling, they radiate spite
when this you read, liable you become
to conspiracy charges filed with their fiendish Goddy

"Scot poet pyschologist who . . ." — R.D. Laing, author of a.o.
"The Bird of Paradise" and "Knots." "rakshasas" — hungry demons.

49

the mouth had that turn that says lucky at cards
unlucky in love   "no hay caminos, hay que caminar"
ah yes all the elegance twisting thro' our murderous empires
and their insistent vibraphone style
it reverberates in the evening air
as we circumambulate the church in Larchant
thirteenth century, burned & ruined for good
in the sixteenth   by one Count Montgomery
former captain of Henri the Second's Scots Guards
after he happens to kill Henri "by mistake"
i.e. by driving a lance through his eye in a tournament
but as Cousin Louis once pointed out
"a man is never martyred in any honest sense
in the pursuit of his pleasure"

"no hay caminos, hay que caminar" — "no roads? keep walking!"
(Sp.). Attributed to St John of the Cross.

50

ah Guillaume this aviation morning
the trees abloom with sirens
along avenues of ancient crimes
airworthy heads sail on slowly
chessmen chesswomen humming rose gas songs
(ah, those upswept hat brims, Goethe, Buffalo Bill)
while squawking bugles herald ragged centurions
risen from elderly fires in frozen starlight
now who could stay linear for more than five seconds
no need to call for cerebral backup
as life growls on through heaped-up space
rubbery distant othernesses
nor is key house but it lets you in
to evening's grace and a cup of coffee

51

yes 'twas an Arcady, le temps both weather and time
tread softly when you sneak across the border
find quiet spot to curl up, gaze
at chance to think
                        in work & think time
on close farness   structures curled back
in vaporous melody of life and lives,
breeze through the grand accordion of frames
watch reflections flounce
prattling selves, quavered elliptics
sink into head's reanimated folds
but don't forget where you keep your heart
and whom the fires have eaten.
mist over arches of invisible speech

52

Finnish word dream   clacks and alliterates:
"kolpakko, kapakka, kalpa"   tankard, tavern, épée
no doubt from early reading
of *The Three Musketeers* in Finnish
with footnotes that said "French pun: untranslatable"
and if I hadn't been born there
that would just be catacomb gibberish
wouldn't you rather dream of
Heidegger's Being and Frankenstein's Monster
hey what's wrong with Heidegger's Being
it's the ing, stupid
but there's not that much wrong
with Frankenstein's Monster, either
only the creature knows its awful secret joys

53

now no more late night city street drives
looking for A Lodging for the Night
at least not for a while   instead
early wet snowy drive home along Sheridan Avenue
big sign facing the road says
"Scoop Chinese Food: One Dollar"
ah Barcelona mornings in the Barrio Gótico
which English are we now speaking
the day and the hour are ends in themselves
said Aleksandr Herzen   not a means
to another day or another experience
a heart moated by joyful pessimism he was
he believed that remote ends were a dream
& that faith in them was a fatal illusion

"A Lodging for the Night" — Cousin Louis's wonderful story
about the great 15th century poet François Villon.

54

joys sorrows but in miniature
candent flinders   none of this heavy stuff
like "tragedy — the protein of consciousness"
don't ask me who said that
fools like me can read the Tarot
but only God can make a carrot
what crowing eccentricity!
the director turns
surveys pale silhouettes
"I'll tell you what to do
while you're waiting for the bus
when the bus comes you're on your own"
legends of grace? sealed & farouche
now slides the silent meteor on

"candent" — glowing from or as if from great heat (first used
by John Clare in 1577). "flinders" — splinters or fragments;
probably of Scandinavian origin. "I'll tell you what to do . . . ":
Ted Berrigan in a Kerouac School workshop, 1978.

55

rebellious servants vandalized the viburnum
but venerable masons tended the heights
now those are timeless lines
from the quill of "poet humorist translator Anselm Hollo"
apostrophized thus by cultural workers
at the Daily Camera a pretty humorous name for a paper
founded back in the days when Rocky Mountain Joe
clambered these steep rocks with tripod & flowing locks
& Oscar Wilde recited the memoirs of Benvenuto Cellini
to Leadville miners ("the most elegant males
in the universe" said Oscar)
& they asked him to bring that Mr. Cellini along next time
when told that the dapper swordsman was dead and buried
in his native Italia they wanted to know "Who shot 'im?"

56

you're born and you grow and as you're growing up
things never quite happen in the right way
and you never get enough of everything
and then suddenly you're a little bit older
and you're getting too much of everything
and then you're quite a bit older
and everything hurts a little
then, alas, you die
                              yes Ted yes it is very much like it
but you are the master of intelligent conversation
and no emotional slither   consummately gentle
stops and starts
                    and rain makes us sad
because it reminds us of the time   when we were fish

The first eight lines are a verbatim quote from Ted Berrigan's
Kerouac School workshop in 1978. Ezra Pound praised Mina Loy's
poems for their "intelligent conversation vs. emotional slither."
"it is very much like it" — Gertrude Stein. "and rain makes
us sad" — Ramón Gomez de la Serna.

57

Just heard myself say
"That's as good as a Guggenheim,
Man!" But can't remember
What it was that was as good as a Guggenheim
Saw Peggy Guggenheim once, in Venice
With her little dogs in white tennis shoes
I mean she was wearing the shoes
But the dogs where nice & white, too
Write write delete delete
Some things there are that are unreadable
Poor Stuart Merrill   to take him out
Of the formaldehyde was a big mistake
But you read his works didn't you? Yes,
I did. And now you've read this, too

58

it was good the labor of building a citadel to the muse
that blows from the green fields and from the clouds
and the result was elevating thoughts
tunnel doodles out of cognition igloo
hope your floorboards settled   why are you mattering?
another speaker figures in you   composted & composed
yet stuck or struck for ever with an English tone or tune
that SOUND hits the EYEBALL — here comes the GHOST!
& as for the omission of essential grammatical elements
essential to whom is the question to ask
why should best minds groan under most distress
asked William Drummond & centuries later
Allen Ginsberg tried to answer that question
sway deep shade opaque   smoke between stars

"it was good . . .": from "The Enemy of the Citadel" by Max Jacob,
as translated by Ted Berrigan. Lines 2 and 3 from Wordsworth,
"The Prelude." "that SOUND hits . . .": "The human eyeball has
a resonant frequency of 18 cycles per second . . . the eyeball may
vibrate in sympathy to low-level waves causing a 'serious smearing
of vision.'" — Guardian Weekly, 16 August 1998.

59

now this is getting a bit noir is it not
back here in the sauvage West
(still such a pretty savage)
but yes we do live in fear of an age
of the absolute rule of absolute greed
for absolute power   (yes of and of)
wielded by bodies that live sans human souls
lumps devouring digesting and being digested
not what the "founding fathers"
(boorish little land "owners" that they were)
had in mind   this is bye-bye America
this is to put it mildly Hell
Cassandra remember her little Cassandra
her wail doth echo in these open spaces

"wielded by bodies . . .": "Now bodies live without the souls of men /
Lumps being digested; monsters in our pride" — George Chapman,
Hymnus in noctem.

60

oie blanche white goose in French "an innocent young thing"
not so young this one but certainly innocent
& not deserving of barbarous funnel torture for liver
distention the Gallic mangeurs so fondly practice
in Nemours supermarket mine eyes beheld a coq au vin
whole chicken crammed into bottle with dim reddish liquid
hail Damien Hirst! thy art doth put one off one's food
if that manner of food it be
nature herself will inform us Tertullian wrote
whether before gross eating and drinking we were not
of much more powerful intellect more sensitive feeling
than when the entire domicile of men's interior is stuffed
with meats inundated with wines and fermenting with filth
pull down thy arrogance French mangeur   pull down

"hail Damien Hirst!": British artist who has exhibited
cross-sections of cow carcasses immersed in formaldehyde.
Tertullian (ca.160-240 CE) quote from his *On Feasting or
Abstinence Against the Carnal-Minded*. "mangeur" — eater (Fr.).

61

impetuous bellows for attention
human or vole they all want attention! want
the gods and goddesses to descend & cuddle
them. yes. well. reality always tough
so we had romantic realism social(ist) realism
surrealism superrealism and they're all the same
mostly poor excuses for getting something down
on canvas paper film and tape
bees above ants ants above worms worms above plants
as above so below yesyes you heard that one before
his helmet now shall make a hive for bees
so why don't you kick nicotine & write some "Clean
and Well Literature" — eh? all right
here's a cookie: go sit in the corner

"bees above ants" etc.: Jain classification, hierarchical according to
number of sensory organs. "his helmet now" — George Peele,
Polyhymnia. "so why don't you . . .": Tom Raworth's book of poems
Clean and Well Lit was listed as "Clean and Well Literature" on the Barnes
and Noble website (10 February 1999). "all right / here's a cookie" —
"You have to recognize the demons, or else they'll annoy you like
mosquitoes. But if you acknowledge their existence, if you say, 'All right,
here's a cookie: go sit in the corner,' then you can go about your work,
and you don't have to go into a deep depression because of it."
— James Broughton, interviewed by Jack Foley on KPFA, 1997.

62

yes Kai by historical happenstance
the jazz saxophone is indeed anglophone
"flying machines is perfect"
but when is that sentence correct
lines and lives to be reinserted
who can wait for the verb as we fly
through the accordion of frames
the if is the yew the holly the houx
"Mr. Andronicus?" "No, it's Sardonicus"
card in wrong slot all pains and sorrows
in miniature let's go visit the foot
how are you foot oh I'm O.K.
I bear the traces impressed on me
by Mr. World and Ms. Life

"yes Kai": Finnish poet Kai Nieminen who rhymed the two words.
"Mr. World and Ms. Life": "I am finally faced only with the following
question: to what extent have I succeeded in transposing into language,
with the greatest precision, the traces impressed on me by world and life?"
— Austrian poet Friederike Mayröcker (Mail Art).

63

has he returned with outrageous opinions?
oh no I find the place as beautiful as ever
apart from its tolerance of Salem's grim offspring
sometimes do wonder about all these folks
with their new houses new cars new children
they are of course willing to shed their blood & others'
in defense of their . . . their way of . . . life . . . ? yes? no?
but I'm glad to have shared some of the century's ride
with Armand the Scholar-Translator of *The Tablets*
his wild tenderness   serious fun   friendly learnedness
& (as the English used to say) "no side"
last painter to stay at the old Chevillon
was the American Walter Palmer   in 1914
"last one out turns off the lights"

"Salem's grim offspring" — the bafflingly resistant vicious strain
of narrow-minded Calvinism that still afflicts U.S. American
political discourse. "Armand" — Armand Schwerner (1927-1999),
author of *The Tablets*, one of the century's major serial poems, in which
he assumes the persona of "the scholar-translator." "last painter" —
of the late 19th/early 20th century crowd at the Hotel Chevillon; since
its renovation in 1994 it has once again become a retreat for artists and
writers. 1914 was, of course, the year World War One began.

64

She of the White Hands flutters with doves
around old Tour de Gannes
on foggy Grez (yes, gray!) mornings
past always more present when elsewhere
FRENCH POET SEES GERONIMO CANTER
                THROUGH JURASSIC PARK
so many places remembered
"the way the road turns
it's special"   trees arching over
on the way to the quarry ponds
in memory's Chinese boxes
you walk along you stop
you have little balloons with question marks
appear above your head
where was that?   was that me?

"She of the White Hands" — Blanche of Castile (1185-1252), queen
of Louis VIII of France and regent during the minority of their son
Louis IX, "Saint-Louis." During the later years of her son's reign she
held court at Grez in a fortified castle whose only remains now are a
few walls and the "Tour de Gannes," a ruined sandstone tower just
off the present rue Wilson. "the way the road turns" — phrase
remembered from Finnish poet Pentti Saarikoski's *Trilogy*.

65

fix some matter, eh? sit down in delight
to further it up   in photon-music's air
an anthology there
of laughing you — will it swell to a movie?
no, no drugs. just a kindly tome
of vintage conundrums submitted to you-all's future
by this morning's super performative
CROCUS   holding up through the afternoon
it's kept me seriously rolling
on with culture & major works
totally unwound   thanks to the French
sing with watery creatures
sleep in leaky boats   be a myth in the land
(let national disgrace proceed apace)

66

graceful awkwardness the mode
most suited to the disarmament of matter
in delirious over-amped atmosphere of Y2K US
the gift to be simple   it lives in a dimple
you don't say yes and it is bound for international
nay intergalactic acclaim
no question   any questions
well then let us recline
on the riverbank and watch
White Mama Goose of Grez
as fubsily majestic
she sails under the bridge
upstream and away
her honk reverberates   in evening air

"fubsy" — chubby & somewhat squat (UK).

Set in **Cochin**.
The Paris foundry of *Ceberny & Peignot*
was the first to release this design in the
early 1900's—under the name *Sonderduck*.
This version, named for 19th century
printer *Nicolos Cochin,* was created in 1977
by Mathew Carter for Linotype.
A favorite loved for its sharp,
ragtime elegance & an italic *joie de vivre.*

Titling is **Goodfellow** from Scriptorium.

~

*book design by **J. Bryan***

Anselm Hollo was born in Helsinki, Finland in 1934 and was educated there and in the United States (he spent his senior year in high school on an exchange scholarship). In his early twenties, he left Finland to live and work as a writer and translator, first in Germany and Austria, then in London, where he was employed by the BBC's European Services from 1958-1967. For the last thirty-three years, Hollo has lived in the United States, teaching creative writing and literary translation at numerous universities including SUNY Buffalo, University of Iowa, and the University of Colorado. He has read his work, lectured, and conducted workshops at universities and colleges, art museums and galleries, literary conferences, coffeehouses, and living rooms.

He is now on the faculty of the Jack Kerouac School of Poetics, the graduate Writing and Poetics department at The Naropa University, a Buddhist-inspired nonsectarian liberal arts college in Boulder, Colorado, where he and his wife, painter, assemblagist, and book artist Jane Dalrymple-Hollo, make their home.

Hollo's poetry has been widely anthologized, and some of it has been translated into Finnish, French, German, Hungarian, and Swedish.

photograph by Michael Friedman